**Binghamton Vet Center**
53 Chenango Street
Binghamton, NY 13901
P: (607) 722-2393
F: (607) 722-0413

# Tanka Practice

**an invitation to
self-reflection
through poetry writing**

**L. Ihde**

## acknowledgments

This book features the poetry of Monika Furch, Nelima Gaonkar, Leslie Ihde, Allison Miller, Ellen Pratt, Valerie Rosenfeld, Michelle Russo and Esra Sarioglu all of whom have participated in tanka practice.

The poetry contained in this book was selected and edited by Leslie and Nelima.

eight souls

find their lines

listening to

what haunts them

they find peace

# Introduction

I don't now remember exactly how I
stumbled upon tanka. Perhaps I was
perusing Amazon's books of haiku,
longing for some succinct form of poetry
that wouldn't be a downer. I had read a
quote that said a novel was a failed short
story and that a short story was a failed
poem. The quote immediately resonated
with me. I found myself reflecting on it.
Was it true? I thought of my clients and
of how together we would search,

conversation after conversation, for the essential articulation of the dilemma they were experiencing. Sometime we would arrive at a sentence that would seem to tell the whole story. This sentence would be like a poem.

Many such sentences have appeared to me during my own search for clarity. I'm a potter, and one such sentence came to me when I was trying to describe what the perfect pot would be. I came up with, "I want to make the pot I didn't make." This obscure, Zen-like remark referred to hours and hours of pottery making: the effort to perfect my craft. It was the culmination of what in retrospect was an exercise in perception. The only pot that could be satisfactory to me would be the one that no longer bore traces of myself.

Tanka is a form of Japanese poetry that predates haiku. Strictly speaking, it is composed of 31 syllables arranged like a haiku with two additional lines of 7 syllables. In other words, 5-7-5-7-7 written in five lines. Modern English tanka doesn't usually emphasize the syllable count but rather rhythm and meter.

Tanka proved to be the perfect poetry form to use as a deliberate practice in self-reflection. In my exploration of this practice I was assisted by several students and friends. Their poetry appears in this book. Witnessing the fruits of their self-explorations you will see how tanka practice can be woven into your life. It is helpful to have a group of like-minded friends, but it is also completely possible to write tanka on your own as a daily meditation.

Our tanka may or may not meet the
technical requirements of tanka
according to some. No matter. We are
putting a premium on perception. We are
hoping for beauty too. For me, as a
psychotherapist, there is nothing more
beautiful than clarity. A sharply defined
sentence reaches from the soul of the
speaker to the heart of the listener. We
are trying to do that.

always bothered

by endless talking

I listened

waiting

for just one word

Of course this is not new, and yet, like every discovery, it is brand new to the discoverer. Awakening again in a new form, the self is born each moment.

We began by writing our intentions each morning and sending them by e-mail to like minded friends. Intentions are our individual plans to live wakefully each day. We concluded the day by sending a commentary on how our day's intentions unfolded. These were written in prose and sometimes became lengthy and emotionally heavy.

In an effort to correct this, we moved to writing poetry. Emphasizing succinctness, honesty and beauty, we found the poetry mutually inspiring. First working in haiku, our practice has since evolved to the writing of tanka.

Tanka writing is a wonderful exercise in perception. Beauty is the natural outcome of succinctness and truth. To begin your own tanka practice, start your morning by writing one. The tanka should be simple, spontaneous and reflect a perception that has struck you. Later you can revise your tanka to develop its artistic attributes.

The most crucial aspect of tanka practice is that you reach deeply within to discover your own inner art. Connecting with your intention each morning can lead to a more powerful day. Sharing those intentions will help you focus your awareness. The others with whom you share silently support your effort.

Your effort to be essential creates a pressure on you to clarify your perceptions. In our opinion, this pressure also helps you write good poetry. These simultaneous actions; self-seeing and ascending to beauty, are at the heart of tanka practice.

I've divided the selected poems into sections related by theme instead of by author. Our poetry expresses experience and perception that we all share as faces of the Self. The true author is this Self. The individuals whose work is seen in this collection listened deeply to the insights that called to them.

There are many tanka poets more experienced than myself - many that I admire. I request their patience as we bend and fold tanka into a deliberate exercise for the modern contemplative. I hope that my experience as a poet and a psychotherapist come together to enrich tanka writing as an aid to self-discovery.

## Family and Friends

Bound by some inexplicable karma, we
touch and are touched deeply by the lives
of our family and friends. As we grow up,
our parents grow older. As we become
mature, we witness their decline. Reading
our fates in their faces, we struggle
against the ropes of life's conditions and
ponder if we can escape or at least learn
from their mistakes. On the other side of
the spectrum, we see the children we
raise. Watching jewel-like hope flower
before us, we experience again the joy of
youth.

the gray in
your hair
the weathered look
your skin has now
~ one day I will be alone


leslie ihde

recoiling from
memories' scorch
even now
the beauty
penetrates


leslie ihde

peels of laughter

erupt from me as little

girls dance playfully on stage

   my infectious joy

    the audience laughs louder


ellen pratt

they've been
tennis partners for years
refining their skills
lobbing back and forth
over the same net


valerie rosenfeld

we see how

we double bind each other

and then sit down

to share

a cup of tea


valerie rosenfeld

after they died

we found the journal

grandma kept

in the attic

our uncle was her favorite


leslie ihde

as we watch our parents

it becomes clear

unlike wrinkles,

wisdom is not a gift of age

but must be sought


monika furch

tape your name

on the dresser

go on sweetie

then they will know

it's for you and not for auction


leslie ihde

I say

I'm not getting married

in a world of

mothers and daughters

things fall apart


esra sarioglu

the gift of
feminist books
when I was fourteen
   a Jesuit priest
   who knew my father


leslie ihde

seeing the past

from this present

I would like to practice

seeing the present

from what lies ahead


leslie ihde

how quickly laughter and awe

turn into tense moments

I resist the urge to smooth things over

seeking redemption

I grasp for truth instead


nelima gaonkar

every word uttered

some kind of request

for her to know me

no sense that my reality

might qualify hers, until now


allison miller

## Change

George Harrison told us that *all things must pass*. If what passes is what we love, we mourn. If what passes brings us relief, we are grateful. If we can transcend our attachments, perhaps we will greet change with more equanimity.

rusts and yellows, damp

scraping against concrete

piling high just after sunrise

one year ago

I raked the leaves of a different tree


michelle russo

metal, manipulated

crafted into a

Bird of Prey

today

I remove you from my neck


michelle russo

brief conversation

with new faces

Beautiful Faces


this is when you disappear

this is when you die



michelle russo

sun rises

light casts its way into a bedroom window

what feels new

may just be

a great continuation


michelle russo

migrating birds

not knowing what will greet them

couldn't stay where they were~

letting go of old representations

simple and difficult


ellen pratt

## Quiet Moments

These are the moments in which we take notice. Perhaps an unexpected thought comes to mind. In the quiet, we neither judge nor avoid. We just notice. In these moments, the tanka we write are the most spontaneous and the most true.

this morning I wake early

not following my usual routine

    instead I sit in front of the fire

    and leave the secret room

    but try to keep the secret


valerie rosenfeld

during the day

words stand still

on a white piece of paper

when I dream at night

words restlessly move in my mind


esra sarioglu

Late at night

I watch the world

from a bus window

until I see the reflection

of my face in the same window


esra  sarioglu

how can three rocks

express my essence when

I cannot speak it?


ellen pratt

like a circle the moon

moves through phases new

to full to new again~

always catching myself

being myself


ellen pratt

I play hide and seek

with myself sometimes forgetting

that I am the one being sought

I look for others instead

and then wonder who's missing


nelima gaonkar

worries in the world

muddled dreams

touching my core

    looking at who I am being

    rethinking my choices


ellen pratt

more and more I feel

the impact of yesterday's

choices today

past and present are fused

~everything matters


allison miller

a familiar look

on a gray cat's face

revealed the attitude of his annoyance~

made me wonder

what are my faces


ellen pratt

questioning

what seems most true

a weight is lifted

finally all objections

fall away


allison miller

being held hostage

by my own darkness

what's the ransom?


allison miller

freshly fallen snow

covers everything

I see my footprints ~

ahead of me is wide open

but steps behind reveal a direction


allison miller

pressed against time

face to glass

peering through the window

trying to find a way in

without becoming part of the display


nelima gaonkar

what's missing at the
conclusion of the day?
awareness lapses
I wander off to seek fullness
that will obscure the lack


nelima gaonkar

a child

with bitten nails

now grown

she scratches her scalp

anxiety not outgrown


esra sarioglu

weekend arrives

still a lot to do

is the frantic pace necessary?

    preparedness is not a substitute

    for presence


nelima gaonkar

leaving the

meditation hall

people wobble as they walk

the ground beneath them

not as solid as before


allison miller

shared immediacy

disguised as closeness

leaves me tired and empty

seeing the ruse

brings me back home


monika furch

## Work

There is always plenty of work to go around. Cleaning, raking, cooking, shopping, sweeping, and office work. If we want to exclude work from our real life we will find our reality pressed into the space of a flimsy weekend or ten minutes of 'my time' with a cigarette or a phone call. Embracing work as an aspect of practice redeems the time spent in life doing what we don't, at first, really want to do. These poems explore work and in some cases, embrace it as an aspect of the mystery and joy of life.

buried by work

all of my choosing

do I still believe

that without the work

I am no one?


monika furch

feeling stopped

I numb myself

dulling the body's impulse to protest

mind frustrated; body complacent

cooperative employee


nelima gaonkar

my attempts to keep

frustration at bay

transport me to a distant realm

      mindless in the here and now

         what good is that?


nelima gaonkar

wind was my partner today

lifting and smoothing

the large plastic sheeting

just long enough for me to fold it

nature's extra hands


nelima gaonkar

slow and steady

eventually I find my way

into the task

and into my body

how nice to discover this is possible


nelima gaonkar

how sweet the almond butter

a few days without sugar

is life always this sweet

     when we don't add anything

     to get away from what is?


nelima gaonkar

my name on a sign

with letters four inches high

bigger than the rest

are they pointing at a dark

truth about me that they see?


ellen pratt

emptying the space

of chaos and garbage

I continue cleaning~

I can't tell where the room ends

and my mind begins


valerie rosenfeld

## There But For Fortune

Many of the poets in this anthology are also
psychotherapists. A strange and privileged life,
the therapist is sometimes the confessor,
sometimes the inadvertent advisor. Perhaps
more often, he or she tries to heal. In the course
of this effort, the therapist sometimes heals him
or herself. At the very least, the therapist
recognizes the common thread of his own trials
and that of his patient. There but for fortune,
go you or I.

awareness store

now open

big awareness

small money

~the pope's indulgences?


strung out addicts

should I tell them

there's a sale

going on now

~look within save big


leslie ihde

in the morning I told my client

it is good to exercise

to get out of moods

in the afternoon I found my way

back to my elliptical


valerie rosenfeld

coffee before dawn
a day of people ahead
    starting in the dark
    we might come to see
    the mysteries we are


valerie rosenfeld

people come to me

in suffering and pain

it's too much

I listen anyway

silence transforming us both


allison miller

I dream of my fears

and wake up with relief

"oh what a dream!"

does God give us nightmares to

show us we can wake up from them?


valerie rosenfeld

playing hide and seek

my enemy

and friend

surely you and I have

travelled this road before


leslie ihde

## Beauty

Sometimes we are struck simply by the way colors work together. An unexpected beauty interrupts our routine and we find ourselves pausing simply to admire. Perhaps these are the quintessential poems.

big yellow quinces

red pomegranates

waiting for

a still-life painter

on my kitchen table


esra sarioglu

two yellow roses

face each other

before the winter

    we walk the empty streets

    everyone sleeps


esra sarioglu

two dalmatian dogs
running with me
on the beach
white sand gray sky
black spots


leslie ihde

bare limbs

against gray sky

slowly

it all becomes clear

dawn reveals gently


valerie rosenfeld

mountain vista

feeling big

not remembering

small

until I see the bluebird


leslie ihde

## Love

Every poem in this book is a love poem. The carefully chosen words are spoken to the heart by the heart. The few poems in this section are love poems to a particular one. Sometimes we are just a little narrow minded.

hot and encompassing

embers grew

just like the red in your eyes

the night we realized

our fate


michelle russo

our dog

all 80 pounds of him

sleeps between us

we touch hands

across a furry divide


leslie ihde

tenderly I note

aging in my husband's face

life's limits known

no need to rush

this sweet time together


leslie ihde

she said her greatest

fear came true

    her mother loved her less

    when she was honest

    ~ I loved her more


allison miller

## The Critical Eye

The critical eye is part of all of us.
Sometimes we are scathing. Sometimes self-
critical. If the self-criticism isn't immobilizing,
we may learn from it.

If our critical eye is turned on the world,
our observations can be sharp and powerful.
When working with our critical eye great care is
required. The following tanka represent our
effort to use critical consciousness with wisdom.

fake orchid in

the dermatologist's reception area

why not a real one?

don't think it's the expense

is it for unreal women?


ellen pratt

feeling distant from my self

and from others

thinking I should be able to shift

to fix this now

I decide to watch carefully instead


monika furch

taking things personally

as if it were all about me

my achilles heel~

I want to save us all

from myself

valerie rosenfeld

## Tanka Strings

We didn't know there were such things as tanka strings, but we discovered them. Later, much to our surprise, we found that not only do they exist, but that they are ancient. We began by conducting dialogues in tanka form. Our tanka strings are usually between two people, the second responding to the first. It is easy to see that the technique can flourish in many directions.

with adeptness the falcon soars

with practice

the student attains mastery

with mastery comes perception

why do I resist practice?


ellen pratt



resisting practice

is practicing resistance

we're all adepts

practicing ourselves

but who is that?


valerie rosenfeld

I throw the shell

into the sea

as if I could return it

    why not

      repair the sand


leslie ihde



my friend's joyful wave

passes over me

I smile with her

    illusory boundaries

      fade like footsteps in sand


allison miller

things look different

after rest

dropping a mood

    sometimes I forget

    everything effects how I see


valerie rosenfeld




dropping a mood~

find the moment

before moods

are born

live there


leslie ihde

I notice a look in my eye

the look has the shape

of disappointment

that the world is as it is

noticing, the shape melts into presence


valerie rosenfeld




while standing on my head

your disappointed eyes

are smiling~

    is there a world as it is

    or a you as you are?


leslie ihde

wanting to be myself

nothing wrong with that

except myself

    I identify

    with this tug of war


valerie rosenfeld


wanting yourself

first mistake

this gesture spawns the rest

    forget right and wrong

    who are you really?


leslie ihde

I tense at the prospect

of a hurried day

yet I know

finding my stride

means relaxing into the race


nelima gaonkar



going back to work

is merely challenging

    what makes it overwhelming

    are the demands

    on my awareness by others


monika furch

waking I try
to quiet my breath
match the morning
stillness
tension is not useful here

nelima gaonkar


burden relieved
by realizing it's my choice
to add one more challenge
　　there is always room
　　for what frees


monika furch

## For Further Information on Tanka

http://www.tankaonline.com

http://www.ahapoetry.com

http://tankasocietyofamerica.com

http://innerartjournal.com

Leslie Ihde lives in upstate New York with her husband and their golden retriever. She writes poetry to mark moments of insight and gratitude. She also edits Inner Art Journal along with Nelima Gaonkar. The journal which publishes short poetry, especially tanka, can be found at www.innerartjournal.com.

Leslie is the author of *Inner Art, Beauty and the Third Eye* which can be found on Amazon.

Made in the USA
Lexington, KY
03 February 2012